MINDFULNESS
FOR
teen
anxiety

MINDFULNESS

anxiety

A PRACTICAL GUIDE TO MANAGE
STRESS, EASE WORRY, AND FIND CALM

JAMIE D. ROBERTS, LMFT

**ROCKRIDGE
PRESS**

For general information on our other products and services or to obtain technical support, please contact our Customer Care Department within the United States at (866) 744-2665, or outside the United States at (510) 253-0500.

Rockridge Press publishes its books in a variety of electronic and print formats. Some content that appears in print may not be available in electronic books, and vice versa.

TRADEMARKS: Rockridge Press and the Rockridge Press logo are trademarks or registered trademarks of Callisto Media Inc. and/or its affiliates, in the United States and other countries, and may not be used without written permission. All other trademarks are the property of their respective owners. Rockridge Press is not associated with any product or vendor mentioned in this book.

Interior and Cover Designer: Richard Tapp
Art Producer: Hannah Dickerson
Editor: Andrea Leptinsky
Production Editor: Ruth Sakata Corley
Production Manager: Jose Olivera

All illustrations used under license from iStock.com and Shutterstock.com

Paperback ISBN: 978-1-63878-382-4
eBook ISBN: 978-1-63878-551-4

R0

For 9-year-old Jamie Danielle, the playful artist who yearned for light and hid from the shadows. Due to her resiliency, determination, and perseverance, I have been able to become friends with my shadow and freely shine this little light of mine.

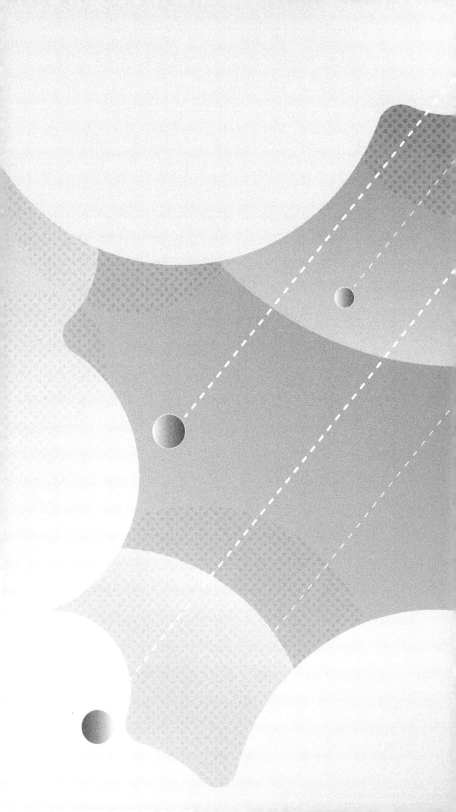

CONTENTS

INTRODUCTION

Did you know one-third of teenagers in America live with an anxiety disorder? If you are one of them, you are definitely not alone! And there are a variety of tools available to help you cope, heal, and have hope.

I am Jamie, psychotherapist, painter, and anxiety connoisseur. I enjoy working with youth your age because I was once like you. In an attempt to understand what was going on inside of me I began studying and practicing psychology. I earned a bachelor of science in psychology from UCLA, then completed a master of science in clinical psychology from Antioch University. As a Licensed Marriage and Family Therapist (LMFT), I've had the privilege of learning and practicing in a wide variety of settings: a community mental health center, a makeshift office in a closet at a middle school, and a private adolescent psychiatry practice. Today, I am the founder of Equilibrium Counseling Services, a teen mental health center. And now I am sharing what I have learned with you.

Become the person you needed when you were young.

—AYESHA SADDIQI

My relationship with anxiety began in third grade and peaked in high school when depression joined the party. When I was in ninth grade, I had my first mental health breakdown. Grades, college applications, career plans, friends, dating, family stuff—it was all too much. I was overwhelmed with racing thoughts and constant "what if" questions popping up in my head. I would stay up all night crying because of the day that had ended and the next one to come. It all felt out of my control. I wanted to withdraw and do nothing. Eventually, I found my footing, changed how I talked to myself, became less critical, slowed down, and started to ask for and accept help. This was not an easy path. But I'm proud to say I've made it. Although my anxiety is not gone, it no longer controls my life. My goal is to help ease this transition as you navigate into the "real world."

Forget the stiff image of a couch and blank walls when you think of therapy. In my practice we are colorful, creative, celebratory of the unique, and welcoming to everyone. My favorite way to connect with my clients is through the use of creative arts; not all emotion can be expressed through words. With paint, you can attribute a color to each emotion. With games, you can learn to set limits and ask for your needs. With music, you can listen to your body and express the words you can't say out loud. You will discover how to connect these unique strategies with mindfulness practices to support the awakening of your authentic self.

This is your book, and you can move through it in any way you'd like. It is important for teen minds to understand why a task needs to be done, how it is performed, and when it's best to use it. In these pages you will learn:

- how to define anxiety and mindfulness.

- how anxiety and mindfulness are connected.

- mindfulness tools and exercises to implement in your life to help decrease and manage anxiety.

As you do your first read-through of the book, review the exercises as a whole to create a strong foundation of understanding. Once you've established familiarity, you can jump around and try different skills. Try to make these exercises a daily habit. Practicing mindfulness is like watering a garden: It must be done repeatedly—not just once!

CHAPTER 1

Anxiety + Mindfulness: A New Way of Thinking

In this chapter you will learn what anxiety is and the foundation of mindfulness.

Forewarning: This chapter has a lot of information, and you can take as much time as you need or revisit as often as you'd like. Read through it and note what stands out to you. If it doesn't make sense the first time, it's okay to read that section again. You can always take breaks and come back; don't overwhelm yourself with too much information. Even then, everything might make more sense once you've had time to think about it. And that can be exciting! Whatever way you best absorb the information, you're doing great.

THE WHO, WHAT, WHERE, WHEN, AND WHY OF ANXIETY

Anxiety can look different for everyone, and it can appear in our lives for a variety of reasons. But one thing anyone with anxiety will tell you is that it is common to feel alone in your struggle. Please know that you are not. More people experience anxiety than you realize.

The good news is that it's possible to find out where *your* anxiety comes from. As Dr. Daniel Siegal of the University of California, Los Angeles says, you have to "name it to tame it." This means it is important to dive in and explore your anxiety to better understand what tools you need to manage it.

Of course, it is difficult to build a relationship with something you can't identify. The first step is to understand the different types of anxiety and how they can appear in your life.

What is anxiety?

Anxiety is an intense, excessive, and persistent worry or fear about everyday situations. Physically, it can show up as your heart pounding, rapid breathing, sweating, and exhaustion.

Anxiety can be a normal feeling in stressful situations, like when you are taking a test or speaking in public. It can become a disorder when a feeling turns obsessive to the point that it disrupts your daily life.

Once anxiety is activated in your brain, it doesn't have to live there permanently. There are tools you can use to reset your brain, calm your nervous system, and tell your body the threat is gone.

Who does anxiety affect?

Any human being on this planet is susceptible to an anxiety disorder. Anxiety does not discriminate based on race, sexual orientation, gender identity, or financial status. But it does show up differently in people's lives.

You do not have to have an official diagnosis of anxiety disorder to identify as having anxiety. Only one in three people suffering from anxiety in the United States today receives an official diagnosis.

Where does anxiety come from, and when?

While anxiety can be a serious issue for some, where it comes from—and when it presents itself—varies by person and situation. Major changes, feelings of discomfort, and trauma are common reasons for anxiety.

People can also be genetically predisposed to anxiety, meaning it runs in your family. Sometimes this is related to brain chemistry, such as a low production or absorption of the feel-good chemicals serotonin and dopamine.

You can start to identify where your anxiety comes from by identifying your triggers—the situations, feelings, or memories—that ignite anxiety.

Why does anxiety exist?

Anxiety is really just your brain's safety mechanism alerting you to harmful or fearful situations. But there are many things the brain can perceive as harmful that in reality will not affect your safety, like feeling embarrassed. This makes it easy to end up living in a constant state of threat and fear.

With self-awareness, you can learn how to listen to your instincts, turn anxiety down, and find calm in everyday life.

ANXIETY TYPES: DIFFERENT FORMS, THEIR TRIGGERS, AND SYMPTOMS

Anxiety is not a one-size-fits-all condition; it can show up in a number of different ways. You may experience one or more types of anxiety, and it is not uncommon for the various types to come and go, changing just as you do. It is helpful to identify how and when your anxiety shows up so you can better target the source. For instance, different times in your life will increase separation anxiety (moving out of home for the first time) or decrease social anxiety (you have a great group of friends). Take a moment to think about what your anxiety feels like right now, and what you may have felt in the past.

 ## Generalized Anxiety Disorder

A consistent feeling of worry, nervousness, fear, or apprehension. There often is not a clearly identifiable reason for the anxiety. Often referred to as baseline, meaning your starting point is simply anxious.

Panic Disorder/Panic Attacks

Panic attacks are intense and extreme. During a panic attack a person feels like they are having severe health issues, such as a racing heart, shortness of breath, or even pain in their chest. The identifying feature is that the attack peaks within 10 minutes, then begins to decrease.

Specific Phobia

A phobia is something that causes so much fear that it is debilitating and we attempt to avoid it at all costs. The most common and specific phobias include a fear of throwing up, being alone, germs, and flying. The difference between a fear and a phobia is the extreme level of distress; not liking flying (fear) versus a complete panic where a person has a meltdown at a slight thought of flying (phobia). The person may be able to see that the fear is not logical, but that does not stop it from existing.

Agoraphobia

Often agoraphobia is thought to be a fear of leaving home, although it is rooted in a fear of not having an escape or ability to get out of a situation. Being in a new or uncomfortable environment may be overwhelming, leading to panic and then fear of being in the place again. This can leave people feeling trapped, so they begin to avoid places and just stay in the safety of their home.

Social Anxiety/Social Phobia

Social anxiety can appear as rehearsing what you say, or second-guessing how you interacted with peers. In a social situation you may stay silent or be more focused on your fearful thoughts than the conversation. Comparatively, social phobia is the complete avoidance of social interaction out of fear of embarrassment or rejection.

☁ Separation Anxiety

Separation anxiety is the fear of being separate from a certain person or people, or the fear of being alone. This may show up as not wanting to stay home alone, or not going into a store by yourself. Some people may need to constantly know where their loved ones are out of fear of something bad happening to them. Some of us need to keep a friend on the phone while we do a task "alone."

Learning to Identify Triggers

A trigger is something that occurs right before an emotion. For example, if you had food poisoning (trauma), you now smell that particular food (trigger) and it makes you want to gag (reaction/emotion). A trigger typically happens right before an increase in emotion or an uncomfortable feeling, like the smell of that food. It is super helpful to know what your triggers are, especially if it is something you are able to prepare for or anticipate. Often, a trigger can be a place, sound, smell, memory, situation, environment, or even a certain person. It's also important to know anxiety does not always have a clear trigger; sometimes we can simply be anxious (see Generalized Anxiety Disorder, page 6).

Can you identify the trigger in the following scenario?

Alex is going out to eat with her family. On the drive there, she notices her heart is racing as she repeats what she wants to order in her head. When it's her turn to order, she whispers to her mom. Her anxiety is too high for her to order herself; she exits to the bathroom, regulates her anxiety, and then rejoins her family.

What do you think triggered Alex's anxiety? Most likely it was a fear of public speaking, which she faced when she had to tell the waiter her order. She anticipated her reaction by practicing in the car beforehand, and attempted to self-regulate in the bathroom after the encounter. With this awareness and additional practice, Alex is on her way to conquering her anxiety and fear of speaking in public.

Sorting Out Your Symptoms

When you're first learning about your anxiety, it can be hard to tell where your uncomfortable feelings are coming from. It might seem like your whole body can be affected at times—and it's true! There are both physical and mental symptoms of anxiety. Physical symptoms are called somatic symptoms, and you experience these in your body. Often there is a direct effect, like "I'm nervous, my stomach hurts." Other times it is less direct, like a racing heartbeat, or feeling your shoulders and back hurt after a stressful day.

Mental or cognitive symptoms have to do with your thoughts: what you think, how you think, and how you act on your thoughts. You likely experience both somatic and cognitive symptoms, yet each person will have a different combination. So while you might experience all-consuming, racing thoughts, a different person may experience a rapid heart rate and avoid other people. Both are valid.

Let's look at some common anxiety symptoms. Keep in mind that you may not experience all of them, and different situations will lead to different presentations of the symptoms.

PHYSICAL/SOMATIC

Racing heart

Stomach pain/nausea

Muscle tension

Back pain

Headache

Leg tapping

Sweaty hands

Pacing

Insomnia

Fatigue/tiredness

Breathlessness

Indigestion

Hot flashes

MENTAL/COGNITIVE

Racing thoughts

Rumination (getting stuck)

Negative self-talk

Repetitive "what if?"
    questions

Replaying events

Intrusive thoughts

Memory flashback

Rigidity

Avoidance

Mind going blank

Being overly aware

Feeling disconnected from
your body

SUPPORT IS HERE FOR YOU

Anxiety can be a lot to handle alone. While the exercises within this book will be helpful, they are not a cure. Please know that there are many people in your life that want to support you. Learning together can be a great way to practice.

Self-Love, Support, and Celebrating You

Taking this first step to acknowledge and work on your anxiety is huge and admirable. It can be difficult to believe you can go from struggling to relief—that's a big leap. Let's change that expectation; rather, let's first aim for neutral, then start to work toward relief. It's cliché, but . . . it is a process. It takes practice and repetition to change your thoughts and behaviors. So, let's make sure to celebrate each step along the way.

Asking for help, support, and encouragement are also great steps to take. By no means do you have to make these changes on your own. Actually, when you have support and others making changes with you, it's more likely to stick! It's like learning a new language; if you have someone to practice with, you will become more fluent.

As you move through this book, take note of the examples you connect with, highlight the exercises that are extra helpful, practice them, then come back and see what new information you pick up as your knowledge and awareness expands. Share what you learn with your family or friends. When you are able to teach it to another person, you truly understand it.

WHEN YOU NEED MORE HELP AND SUPPORT

There are endless types of therapy available to you. In this book, you will be introduced to a few skills from each of the top forms of treatment for anxiety, in addition to mindfulness.

Cognitive Behavioral Therapy (CBT)

Developed by Dr. Aaron Beck, CBT focuses on thought patterns that influence behavior. If we change our thoughts and beliefs, we can alter our behavior.

Dialectical Behavioral Therapy (DBT)

DBT, developed by Dr. Marsha Linehan, merges aspects of CBT and mindfulness. It has a heavier focus on emotion regulation to challenge thoughts and behaviors.

Strength-Based

A strength-based therapy method uses positive psychology to develop and focus on your natural strengths rather than your weaknesses.

Narrative Therapy

This type of therapy looks at the story you tell yourself about you and the world around you. This story influences your interpretation of everything. You are the author—what story are you telling?

Each of these therapy modalities will work well for anxiety, but finding what works specifically for you is important. While you will learn skills here, it is important to know when it is time to seek support from a professional. If your anxiety is limiting you from participating in daily life, if the symptoms continue to increase, or if you become fearful of hurting yourself or others, it is time to give a therapist or crisis line a call. In the Resources section of the book there are clear, step-by-step instructions for seeking additional support.

The secret of change is to focus all of your energy not on fighting the old, but on building the new.

—SOCRATES

MINDFUL ANXIETY QUIZ

BENEFIT: *Getting to know your anxiety*

TIME: *10 minutes*

GOAL: *Identify your triggers*

Getting to know your anxiety and spending time with an uncomfortable emotion can be difficult. But the better you know your triggers, the more targeted your mindfulness practice can become.

In this multiple-choice quiz, you will begin to identify the who, what, where, when, and why of your anxiety. Circle all that apply or add a situation that is specific to you. Do not judge or criticize yourself based on what you do or do not answer. There are no wrong answers—we are just gathering information. You can even come back in a month or two with a different color pen to see what has changed. Then as you move forward, you can adjust or continue your mindful practice. This will become your starting point to reflect on how much progress you have made.

1. **Who are you typically with when you feel triggered?**

   Parent/guardian

   Friends

   Strangers

   Siblings

   Authority figure

   Other: _____

2. **Who are you typically with when you feel calm?**

   Parent/guardian

   Friends

   Strangers

   Siblings

   Authority figure

   Other: _____

3. **What tends to increase your anxiety?**

   Being alone

   Too many people

   People you don't know

   Peer pressure

   New places

   Academics

   Loud noises

   Memories

   Physical contact

   Certain people/places

4. **Where do you typically feel anxious?**

School classroom

School lunchroom

Home

In public

Restaurants

Stores

Open spaces

Crowded spaces

5. **When do triggers typically occur?**

Morning

Afternoon

Evening

Night

Sleeping

All the time

Daily

Weekly

Monthly

MINDFULNESS: YOUR NEW ANXIETY-REDUCING BFF

Mindfulness is the practice of being present in the here and now. It is slowing down and taking in aspects of your surroundings, internal sensations, and emotions. It is investing time and energy with thoughtful intention. In this high-speed world, it can be easy to get caught up in mindless thought and action *cough, scrolling social media*. It is okay to still do those activities, but by adding mindful intention, you can enjoy the experience instead of being sucked in.

The Power of Mindfulness

Mindfulness has the power to change your life by helping you recognize, engage in, and influence how your mind takes in and processes information. When partaking in mindfulness, you grant yourself the power to choose your experience. You are in charge and get to dictate how mindfulness works for you. While mindfulness will not make anxiety disappear, it will allow you to determine the level of influence anxiety will have over you. For example, if you are listening to music, you have power over the volume and can determine if the music is a background sound or the main event. It is the same with anxiety; you cannot stop a trigger from happening, but you can learn to control how loud the anxiety is and how long it lasts.

The influence of mindfulness will enter all aspects of your life. You may be learning this skill specifically for anxiety, but the beauty of it is that it will also help with anger, sadness, relationships, studying, and creativity. Others will notice the change in you, and like a ripple effect, mindfulness has the power to spread and help everyone around you. Not only are you decreasing the anxiety, but you are also increasing acceptance and your capacity to handle other situations that impact you on a daily basis.

The Purpose of Mindfulness

The purpose of mindfulness is to increase your self-awareness in all areas of life in order to harness the ability to soothe and comfort your anxiety. Much of life is filled with passive routines and habits. During your morning routine, how well do you pay attention to each action? What would it be like to start your day with purpose, even if you don't want to wake up that early? For instance: noticing the temperature of the water when you rinse your face, the taste of the toothpaste, or the feel of the sweatshirt you choose to wear. Each has influence over how your day begins, and you have control over each one. Therefore, the purpose of mindfulness is to awaken your awareness for your present experience.

What is meaningful, or mindful, to one person may not be received with the same feeling by another. Yet that is the beauty of mindfulness—you get to determine the purpose and make it your own experience.

⚙ The Practice of Mindfulness

Building your mindfulness skills will take time and practice. You can't become a power lifter in one day simply from reading a book about it. You have to practice it repetitively and put it into action. The easiest way to practice mindfulness is by adding it into your daily life, so it becomes a normal part of your day. For example, you could practice mindfulness when you arrive home from school and are greeted by your pet. Before all else, the two of you could sit together sharing scratches and purrs for a moment, feeling right with the world. Mindfulness is not about the length of time; it is about the positive feelings created in a moment.

Ideally, if you are doing things every day that decrease anxiety, even when you aren't anxious, your anxiety will automatically decrease over time. If you only use mindfulness in a crisis, you may forget the skills or become rusty. As you move through this book, take note of the exercises that seem simple enough to do regularly. Try to be mindful every day. Keep doing the skills that support you and help you feel good.

MEANINGFUL MINDFULNESS: THE SEVEN PILLARS

In the 1970s Dr. Jon Kabat-Zinn, a professor of medicine at the University of Massachusetts Medical School, began to study the practice of Buddhist meditation. During his studies he was introduced to the concept of mindfulness, which has been noted as a quality of Zen Buddhist meditation since the fifth century BCE. He began to do research on the healing properties of mindfulness in relation to stress and anxiety. Later, he brought mindfulness to Western medicine through the Mindfulness-Based Stress Reduction program. In the program he highlights the seven most important teaching points of mindfulness.

Non-judging

The human brain is programmed to categorize things as positive, negative, or neutral. Doing so does not really work since most of life is a beautiful rainbow of options. For example, you might think "If I don't get an A, then I'm a failure." Using a non-judging approach, the aim is to acknowledge people/things/situations as they are, without criticism. This approach would include "Getting a B is also a good grade." With mindfulness, you begin to notice when you enter into judgment and when you are able to step back and recognize all of the possibilities.

Patience

Patience is being able to wait for something to unfold in its own time. This can be an extra challenge for the teen brain since the reward center of the maturing brain is typically in charge. This means anything with instant gratification and positive feedback is usually the priority: notifications, likes, or leveling up in a game. Imagine you are waiting for a response from your friend and begin to feel anxious the longer you go without hearing from them. Increasing your patience allows you to recognize that your timeline is not everyone's timeline. There may be a number of reasons why your friend has not yet responded and none of them could be about you.

Beginner's Mind

This is a method of approaching situations as though it is your first time doing so. With anxiety, there is a tendency to make up stories about what may or may not happen, what we call the "what ifs." In reality, you don't know what will happen, and the stories just increase your anxiety and fears. With a beginner's mind, you are in the present moment as it is actively unfolding, experiencing the beauty of newness. When you attempt to anticipate everything that might happen, you can get stuck in your fear-based story and not the reality of the situation. There is safety in anticipating triggers, but it is important to find the right balance that works for you.

Trust

Mindfulness is learning to trust yourself, your internal compass, intuition, feelings, needs, and wants. When you put on a mask and pretend to be someone else, or say you like something that you don't, you dismiss your true self. No one knows you better than you, and if you listen closely, you might already know parts of your truth. The goal is to increase your self-awareness, build confidence in your own experience, and trust that you know what to do.

Non-striving

Almost everything you do is for a purpose or to achieve an intended outcome and has an expectation attached to it. Mindfulness encourages an intention of non-striving; "No goal other than yourself, allow everything you experience from moment to moment to be here." Ideally, it frees you from the expectations of "Am I doing it right?" or "I'm not good at it." Simply the fact that you are engaging with mindfulness is enough. You are enough.

Acceptance

Acceptance comes with seeing the present as reality and believing it as truth. People will show you who they are by their words and actions. When you deny and resist this fact, you begin functioning in a made-up story. Accept that what is presented to you is truth and save yourself the stress of reading between the lines. You also need to accept that what is true in this moment may change as the situation evolves. No feeling lasts forever. This does not mean you should accept negative treatment. If something does not align with your truth, trust in your intuition and set a limit.

Letting Go

This is your ability to release expectations and move forward with what is. When you hold on to a past interaction, it follows you around and influences your present and future experiences. That embarrassing thing you said in front of your friends two years ago is taking up valuable brain space. By letting go, you free up your ability to be in the present. What is done is done and you cannot change it. I encourage you to take note of the number of situations in which you attempt to control the outcome. How much anxiety does it create? Does it give you peace? What would letting that go look like?

GET READY TO GET MINDFUL

Take a breath, and slowly let it out. It is a lot of information, but now that you know it, you know it! So let's start to put it into practice. The following chapters break mindfulness down into four areas: emotions, thoughts, body, and behaviors. Everything is interconnected and can feel difficult to sort out. There is a tendency to clump it all together, which adds to the overwhelmed feeling. Looking at each situation or item separately allows you to identify the main ingredients, and more directly target your mindfulness practice.

Everything's Connected: Your Emotions, Thoughts, Body, and Behaviors

It is impossible for an emotion to arise without being attached to a thought. Your body automatically reacts to your emotions and thoughts, even if they are nearly imperceptible, which impacts the way you behave and how you feel physically. All of it happens in a split second, and it may feel like it is out of your control because it happens so quickly. However, with mindfulness, you can change how your emotions, thoughts, body, and behaviors influence each other. A reaction is an immediate impulse, such as snapping at your sibling for taking your phone charger. A response is a chosen, intentional acknowledgement of a regulated emotion: "I need my charger back."

For example, imagine that you are sitting in class. The teacher asks a question, and they look around the room for someone to call on. The following are likely connected components of the event:

- Emotion: Fear

- Thought: *"I'm going to have to speak in front of everyone."*

- Physical reactions: Dry mouth, heart racing

- Behaviors: Looks down, doesn't make eye contact, fidgety

EMOTION ➔ THOUGHT ➔ BODY ➔ BEHAVIOR

TIPS & TRICKS

The first time you try an exercise, it may not fit quite right and that's okay. Give it another go and see if you can ease into it. Try an exercise for the first time when you are feeling "okay." It's not recommended to attempt a new exercise in the middle of a panic attack. Eventually you can use mindfulness during such an occasion, just not the first time. Think of the exercises in this book like trying on shoes: some are for everyday use, some for specific occasions, and others only for use at home.

For example, Damon wears a sensory fidget ring to help regulate while in class (see Personal Toolbox Exercise, page 100). At home, Damon stretches in the mornings while doing a body scan to connect with his body (see Body Scan Exercise, page 52). When anxiety becomes a bit too much, Damon steps outside to practice breathing exercises (see 5 x 5 x 5 Deep Breathing Exercise, page 46).

The more you put the information within this book into practice, the more in tune you will become with your needs. You can even modify things to fit YOU better. In one of the following exercises I suggest coloring, but if drawing fits you better, go for it! The most important part of engaging in mindful practice is a clear intention of bringing awareness to the present moment.

MINDFULNESS EXERCISE: NOTICING THE NEUTRAL

BENEFIT: *Paying mindful attention to feeling neutral*

TIME: *10 minutes*

The brain is quick to notice the negative or what you don't like. When everything feels negative, it can seem impossible to notice anything positive. So instead, let's highlight the neutral things that are neither good nor bad. In this exercise you will review your day and take notice of moments that were neutral, okay, or fine. The more attention you pay to the "okay" moments, the more you will notice it's not all bad.

1. Pause what you are thinking about and review the day you just had.

2. Notice any interactions or moments that stand out. Set them aside in your mind.

3. What occurred in between those moments? Consider the mundane and typical daily activities that do not bring up extreme feelings (either positive or negative).

EXAMPLES

Your phone has over 50 percent charge.

Your sibling sits next to you and doesn't say anything.

That specific hoodie is clean (enough).

Realizing you don't have homework tonight.

Doing so will bring mindful attention to what is already a part of your day that does not trigger anxiety.

4. Are there moments that happen daily or regularly? If there are, make a note to yourself to pay attention tomorrow when they occur.

5. If you cannot think of something, pay close attention throughout tomorrow and try the exercise again.

MINDFUL COLORING EXERCISE

BENEFIT: *Relaxing your brain*

TIME: *Up to 30 minutes*

Did you know that coloring lights up the same part of your brain as meditating? It does! Mindfulness isn't always words and thoughts; it is also the soothing actions you take to relax your mind. Making art and being creative are great ways to tune into your body and connect with your emotions. Silent meditation is *not* for everyone.

1. Grab your tools: paper, pencils, crayons, coloring book, and paint.

2. Find a comfortable, quiet spot to sit where you can relax and breathe easy.

3. Feel the texture of your seat and the way it supports your body.

4. Looking at your sheet of paper, and notice the blankness.

5. Examine the color options of your drawing tools. Do the colors represent something to you?

6. Grab your first pen, marker, crayon, or pencil. Press it to the paper and feel the texture transfer.

7. As you draw, notice any smells. What does your nose sense? Take in the air with a big inhale, then slowly exhale.

8. Let loose and go for it! Mark up your page with funky colors or go outside of the lines. Give yourself permission to not be perfect.

Try this after a long day at school after overworking your left/logic brain with facts, numbers, and rules. The act of coloring, drawing, or doodling engages the right brain, giving your logical side a break. This will bring a sense of balance.

CHAPTER 2

The Mind – Body Connection

Now let's explore the specific connection between your body and mind. It may be easy to think that anxious thoughts cause your body to experience the anxiety, but in reality, your body sends a signal to your mind when it senses danger, sparking anxiety. Fortunately, your body is also the solution. In this section you will learn about the body's automatic reactions, how to track the triggers, and ways to engage your body in the healing process. Some of the exercises may feel funky or odd the first time, but give them a few tries, and you'll notice a shift in your experience.

LISTENING TO YOUR BODY'S LANGUAGE

Your body is your first home. It houses your mind, and carries you through your day. It is a lovely concept to trust your body and always listen to your gut or intuition. But, especially with anxiety, there are disconnects between your mind and your body. Your body may send a warning signal when, in fact, all is safe. Building communication between your mind and body through mindfulness will increase your ability to trust and listen to your own needs. The best way to do this is by building habits into your everyday routine. The good news is that it's easy to do! Simple activities like a few minutes of movement, drinking water, and getting the right nourishment can make a big difference.

Have you ever forgotten to eat breakfast, skipped school lunch, and then felt irritable and *hangry* when you got home? When you do not fuel your body, it does not have the resources to manage the expectations of the day. This is what it looks like to not listen to your body's needs.

When your anxiety keeps you up at night and you only get a few hours of sleep, it snowballs into anxiety that is even harder to manage the next day. There are times that your safety and physical needs are out of your control, like access to food/shelter, or a younger sibling crying in the next room. There are ways you can check in with your body as a foundation to mindfully manage your anxiety. We'll take a look at these in the upcoming exercises.

Another piece of the mind-body puzzle is how your body experiences anxiety. Chapter 1 explored the common physical symptoms of anxiety. In this chapter you will learn to tune into your body's reactions when triggers present themselves and respond to them with loving care and respect. Things like sweaty hands, stomach aches, or racing heart beats can feel intense! But they're just your body's way of raising a red flag. This chapter will help show you how to calm and reassure your body when that happens. You can also use these exercises to gauge when your anxiety is decreasing. This is similar to how your body tells you what is wrong. Your body is also a tool for healing!

MINDFUL EATING EXERCISE

BENEFIT: *Being present while nurturing your body*

TIME: *10 minutes*

For this exercise you will use your five senses to explore an orange (or any food item). Sight, smell, taste, touch, and sound are your natural ways of connecting with the world around you. This exercise is an awesome way to integrate your mind and body to create a mindful eating practice. Time to explore an orange with guided mindfulness and your five senses.

1. Grab an orange. (Consider freezing it for added effect.)

2. Look at the orange, its shape and color. Feel the texture of the outer peel.

3. Smell the aroma.

4. Squeeze it. Do you hear anything?

5. Begin to peel the outer skin off of the fruit. Do you hear it tear? Does it get under your nails? Do you feel or see juice emerge? Does it feel sticky? What does it taste like?

6. Tear open the fruit, see the white fibers between the slices. The aroma likely smells stronger now. Is it sweet or sour? Does the inside of the orange feel different than the outside?

7. Take a slice of orange and place it in your mouth. Hold it there for a second. How does the taste change? What does it feel like against your tongue? Bite down. Does the taste change? Do the juices flow out? As you continue to chew, how does the experience change?

8. Feel free to continue to explore the fruit with your five senses. What else do you notice?

Try this exercise with other foods! You'll become more conscious of the foods you eat and how your enjoyment increases when eating them.

TENSE AND RELEASE EXERCISE

BENEFIT: *Connecting to your body in an intentional way*

TIME: *5 minutes*

It is important to explore and know your body if you intend to have a mind-body connection. Muscles are a large component of your body, making up 30 to 50 percent of it. Everyone has muscles, whether you can see them or not. In this exercise, you are going to try to flex and release your muscles. Because of anxiety, you may feel muscle pain from tense shoulders, back pain, or muscle cramping. The act of intentionally relaxing a muscle allows the pent-up tension to be released.

This exercise will lead you through a step-by-step mindful body relaxation technique.

1. Find a comfortable place to sit, and focus on your right calf muscle or any large muscle.

2. Point your toe and flex the muscle, holding it for five seconds. Feel the tension build and notice the engagement of surrounding muscles.

3. Release the muscle and relax your ankle. Do you feel the relaxation, the loose limpness of your leg?

4. Repeat two more times. Tense for five seconds, release for five seconds.

5. Try other large muscles, like the quad, forearm, and bicep.

6. You can do this in moments you choose to relax AND in the moment your anxiety increases, in order to redirect your mind to a part of your body you can control in the here and now.

If you shake your leg constantly under your desk, try slowing it down to flex and release your calf muscle. This brings conscious awareness to the motion and creates a soothing feeling.

UNDERSTANDING FIGHT, FLIGHT, OR FREEZE

Now that you have a better idea of how to listen to your body, pay attention to what it's telling you to do.

When a moment of panic or anxiety sets in, humans enter "fight, flight, or freeze" mode. Think of a deer running across a highway and into oncoming traffic. Once they see the headlights, they panic and become paralyzed with fear. Similarly, your brain's autonomic nervous system perceives triggering situations coming and adjusts your fear responses.

The space between calm moments and triggering moments is considered neutral.

When you are triggered, "fight" moments can look like anger, frustration, and yelling. "Flight" moments can look like running away or hiding from people. "Freeze" moments can look like depression, isolation, and exhaustion. Your nervous system chooses these reactions in the moment. Think of a lion's incredible roar, or a gazelle's superfast speed. They happen in an instant!

Fortunately, it is possible to track and pay attention to when and how your body sends these signals.

When you are not in fight, flight, or freeze mode, you are ideally in a neutral state. Dr. Daniel Siegel calls this state "the window of tolerance," where one can tolerate frustrations or annoyances without extreme reactions. In the Mindful Anxiety Quiz (page 14), you practiced noticing when you felt neutral.

This was to give you an idea of what your window of tolerance looks like. Keep in mind that your window of tolerance may shift and change daily, based on your circumstances and self-care.

With anxiety and depression, you can find yourself getting stuck in fight, flight, or freeze mode and struggling to find neutral. Practicing mindfulness will help you know when you are feeling off-balance. With awareness, you can put your skills to use, acknowledge triggered responses, and support your nervous system back to equilibrium.

FIGHT, FLIGHT, OR FREEZE QUIZ

BENEFIT: *Knowing your common responses*

TIME: *5 minutes*

Now you'll take a look at how your triggers spark your fight, flight, or freeze moments.

As you read through this quiz, know that you are not alone in experiencing these moments. If you feel overwhelmed while thinking or working through this exercise, don't be afraid to stop and do the following:

- Take deep breaths

- Move to a place where you can relax and feel safe

- Reach out to a loved one or friend

- Go for a walk to move your body

While you cannot stop your nervous system from reacting, with awareness, you can choose a response.

1. Think of a moment when you were triggered.

2. Do you feel the same emotion now just thinking about it?

3. Which of the following statements can you identify with?

Fight

I become angry suddenly when something doesn't go as I anticipated.

I might yell when I am uncomfortable.

I notice I argue more intensely when I am overwhelmed.

When I feel out of control I get really frustrated.

I firmly and adamantly resist change.

Flight

When I am triggered by a situation, I walk away.

If my anxiety turns to panic, I have to remove myself.

I tend to avoid triggering social situations.

When the pressure is too much, I quit.

When I am overwhelmed in a conversation, I disengage or zone out.

When someone upsets me, I immediately end the interaction.

Freeze

I notice I am silent in difficult situations.

When I am triggered, my mind goes blank.

When life is too much, I stay in bed.

To not be triggered, I avoid most things.

I would rather be alone when I am triggered.

5 X 5 X 5 DEEP BREATHING EXERCISE

BENEFIT: *Regulating internal emotions*

TIME: *3 minutes*

Breathing is a primary mindfulness skill that's been mentioned a few times, so let's talk about why and how it is helpful. Aside from keeping you alive, intentional breathing is a great tool to reset your nervous system and calm anxious feelings. When your nervous system is triggered and anxiety is on the rise, you might feel like you are holding your breath. It can be difficult to think of a calming exercise to implement in the moment. Taking a solid deep breath and holding it for a brief time can slow down a racing heart and release feel-good chemicals called endorphins. Specifically, try using the 5 x 5 x 5 method: 5 seconds in, hold for 5 seconds, and then 5 seconds out.

1. Slowly take in air through your nose for a count of 5, 4, 3, 2, 1. Feel your chest fully expand and air reach deep into your stomach.

2. Hold your breath for a count of 5, 4, 3, 2, 1.

3. Release the air through your mouth for a count of 5, 4, 3, 2, 1.

4. For added benefit, repeat 5 times.

Feeling playful? Grab a bottle of bubbles and try blowing fast, then slow, then just right. Notice how your breath control matters in creating a good bubble? Try to use the same steady focus in the 5 x 5 x 5 breathing exercise.

MIND-BODY AND ANXIETY

You now know why your body reacts with fear or anxiety, and how to recognize when it shows up by tracking your body. So, how can you use your body to help calm the feeling of anxiety? The action of controlling your emotions is called *regulating*. Think about it in terms of temperature. A thermometer reads what the temperature is in a space, and an air conditioner regulates and controls what the temperature in the room will be. When tracking your emotions, you are reading what they are in the moment. When you regulate your emotions, you have the power to change them. The following exercises will teach you how to harness the skills you already have so you'll be prepared to use using them.

The simplest and most direct way to regulate is through *grounding*. No, it is not like when you get in trouble and are grounded for the weekend. Grounding is connecting to the floor beneath your feet, whether it is grass, carpet, concrete, or just your shoes. When your mind starts to spin on a worry, place your feet firmly on solid ground. This will instantly bring you back to the physical here and now. Using your five senses is a great way to become grounded in your body and in the present moment.

How do you implement mindfulness when the situation is out of your control, you can't exit, or your safe space is out of reach? You will need to find your internal *calm place*. Your calm place is the image of a real location you have visited, somewhere you dream of going, or it can be out of this world. It is an environment that is truly relaxing and safe. Start to think of where this may be. Can you visualize the details, colors, sounds, and smells? My calm place is my patio, sitting cross legged as the sun is setting, a slight breeze rustling the trees, my kitten curiously exploring the plants, and for a moment, everything is still and right in the world. What about you? Where is your calm place?

GROUNDING EXERCISE

BENEFIT: *Decreasing anxiety through physical and emotional connection*
TIME: *10 minutes*

Pets are a great way to practice your grounding skills. A cat's purr vibrates at a frequency that is proven to lower stress. Pets are pure of heart with lots of love to give.

Use this exercise to not only connect to an animal but to create and memorize your "calm place." Have you noticed that animals have a natural sense of knowing when you need love? In this exercise you will pay mindful attention to your senses as you connect to the experience in both mind and body. Grumpy, venomous, or water pets are not recommended for this activity.

1. Go to where your pet is or call them to you. Do not forcefully move them.

2. Set an intention to be fully present with your pet for the next 10 minutes.

3. *Feel* the texture of their fur.

4. *Observe* the color and pattern of their coat.

5. *Listen* for any sounds: panting, purring, scratching, or licking.

6. Do they have a distinct *smell*? (Beware of their breath.)

7. Notice how you feel. Has your heart rate shifted? Have your thoughts stopped wandering? Are your shoulders relaxed?

8. Remain present in the activity for a few more moments and simply enjoy.

You can use the details of this moment as a visualization in the future. If you are experiencing anxiety at school, imagine sitting with your pet and moving through your senses with them.

BODY SCAN EXERCISE

BENEFIT: *Physical relaxation and self-appreciation*

TIME: *5-10 minutes*

Body scans are a wonderful and simple way to guide your mind and body to a calm and safe place. In these precious moments, nothing else exists. Find a comfortable place to sit or lay, close your eyes, and enjoy. Read through the following meditation so you are familiar with the flow, then guide yourself through the dialogue using the relaxation techniques you have learned so far. If you can do it with your eyes closed, it will help eliminate external distractions, but having your eyes closed is not essential. These are great at bedtime when you are struggling to fall asleep.

1. Imagine a bright ring of light floating above your head. As the ring slowly moves down and encircles the top of your head, notice your forehead relax.

2. As it moves over your eyes, feel the heaviness of your eyelids and allow tears to flow if they are present.

3. The light moves over your cheekbones and mouth as you unclench your jaw.

4. When it reaches your neck, feel free to turn your head from side to side for a stretch.

5. The light continues on to your chest as you take a deep breath, feeling your lungs expand and contract. Can you feel your heartbeat?

6. The light is now at your waist. Release the fear in the pit of your stomach.

7. As the light reaches your hips and bottom, feel the seat supporting your body. Allow your quads to flex and release as they settle in.

8. The light is moving down your shins to your ankles. Give them a twist.

9. Wiggle your toes and feel the ground under your feet.

10. The ring of light now moves back up your body, acknowledging and appreciating each part of you and refilling you with self-love.

11. As the ring reaches the crown of your head, feel the lightness flow through your body.

CHAPTER 3

Shifting Thoughts

Becoming familiar with your thought patterns can be a bit trickier than becoming familiar with your physical reactions. Our brains are highly developed and intricate, and there is a whole spectrum of how and why you think the way you do.

In this chapter we will explore the foundation of thoughts, how they show up in the teen mind today, and tools for acknowledging, accepting, and shifting your thoughts.

WHAT IN THE WORLD IS YOUR BRAIN THINKING!?

It is impossible to talk about your thoughts without including key information about the brain. In early humans, the brain functioned to keep track of what might kill them. They didn't need to track the safe things because they were not a threat. Instead, the brain had to be constantly assessing threats: poisonous berries, polluted water, and predators. Your modern-day brain is still wired to seek out and remember the negatives, which is why it can be so difficult to remember a compliment and easy to recall a criticism. Through your mindfulness practice, you will learn to notice, identify, and hold on to neutral and positive thoughts as well.

The brain grows and develops until you are in your mid-20s. As a teenager, your brain relies on the amygdala for decision-making and reason, as the prefrontal cortex has not fully formed. The amygdala is also known as the "reward center" of the brain. This means that you are more likely to respond to your instincts, instant gratification, and anything pleasurable, such as video games. Instant gratification, or "wanting it right now," can contribute to anxiety by increasing disappointment when a situation, need, or want is not met immediately. Any delay in relief actively intensifies anxiety and can lead to that feeling of being out of control. The last area of the brain to complete development is the prefrontal cortex, which oversees executive function. This is a mental skill set that includes abilities such as planning, organizing, logic, and impulse control: all the things that teens are often criticized for struggling with. As you grow and mature, you will continue to develop and harness these skills with more ease.

Once you know what the thoughts are that throw you off and increase your anxiety, you have the power to change them. This skill is called "reframing." Picture two separate window frames next to each other. If you look out of each window, you can see the same scene, although from a slightly different angle. Sometimes simply having a new perspective can create a whole new outlook on the situation. Let's explore alternative perspectives and outcomes when reframing negative thoughts.

The moment you have a certain thought and believe it, you will experience an immediate emotional response. Your thought actually creates the emotion.

—DAVID D. BURNS, MD

 S.T.O.P. EXERCISE

BENEFIT: *Early identification of anxious thoughts*

TIME: *3 minutes*

Before you start, be sure to STOP! The earlier you notice your thoughts and anxiety spiraling out of control, the more likely you are to be able to implement your mindfulness tools. The goal is to S.T.O.P. and create a moment for you to choose your response versus reacting spontaneously. This is a great exercise to do in the moment. It will help you practice how to identify and understand your thoughts when they pop up and surprise you. You'll learn to increase your awareness in neutral moments to have a better understanding of your baseline, or neutral starting point. You can add this to your toolbox of skills to use in the moment of an anxiety trigger to change the direction of your thoughts.

While this exercise is great in the moment when your anxiety skyrockets, it's also useful in resolving anxiety lingering from the past. Think of a situation from the last month that made you feel super anxious. Do those same physical symptoms show up for you? Now, move through the four steps of S.T.O.P. to calm your anxiety.

S: Stop what you are doing.

> Put down your phone.
> Pause a conversation.
> Set down your pen.

T: Take a few breaths.

> Try the 5 x 5 x 5 Deep Breathing Exercise (page 46). Breathe in for 5 seconds, hold for 5, breathe out for 5.
> Try it 5 times!

O: Observe the moment.

> Take in information surrounding you: who, what, where, when.
> Note your thoughts in the moment. This is a checklist of facts, not interpretation.
> Take an inventory of how your body is responding: heart rate, pain, position, etc.
> What emotions are being experienced (anger, sadness, fear, disgust, surprise)?

P: Proceed with what will support you most in moving forward.

> Reach out to a friend.
> Walk away from a conflict.
> Start another self-care activity.
> Tell someone what is bothering you.

DYSFUNCTIONAL THOUGHT RECORD EXERCISE

BENEFIT: *Challenging your brain to think about a situation differently*

TIME: *10 minutes*

For this exercise you will use a thought journal to identify negative thoughts and then list alternative neutral thoughts. Think of a situation that often causes anxiety. What is the automatic negative thought that pops into your head? Can you think of an alternative thought that is more neutral? Then try a positive thought. The intention of this exercise is to acknowledge a negative thought and present a possible alternative thought.

1. Grab a pen or pencil and a sheet of paper.

2. Think of a situation that often causes you distress.

    On a scale of 0 to 100, how intense is this situation?
    Write this down.
    Example: You send a text to your friend. They "leave you on read" and don't respond. The intensity of the situation might be 60/100.

3. Feel the *emotion* that comes when you think of the situation.

    On a scale of 0 to 100, how intense is this feeling?
    Write this down.
    Example: You may feel hurt by the lack of response. So, you would write 80/100.

4. Acknowledge the negative *thought* connected to the situation and emotion.

    On a scale of 0 to 100, how likely is this thought to be true?
    Write this down.
    Example: *"They don't actually think of me as a friend."* You might write 40/100.

5. Think of an alternative *reason* the situation may have occurred.

    On a scale of 0 to 100, how likely is this alternative to be true?
    Write this down.
    Example: *"Maybe they were distracted and forgot."* You might write 70/100.

Aim for a neutral alternative thought, then aim for a positive thought. Remember that it is difficult to go straight from negative to positive.

TYPES OF THOUGHTS

Sometimes it may feel like our thoughts are a never-ending stream of useless chatter. The truth is that our most useful thoughts are typically silent.

According to Mo Gawdat, former chief business officer of Google X, there are three types of thoughts:

Insightful thoughts appear when problem solving.

Experiential thoughts appear when focusing on a specific task.

Incessant thoughts are the useless thoughts that feel like mind chatter.

The thing is, when your brain is provided limited information about a situation, it attempts to fill in the blanks on its own. Given that the brain is always on the lookout for threats, it tends to fill in the blanks with a negative or worst-case scenario. Consider it a story your mind is telling you with the intent to keep you safe, although it often turns into anxiety. Another way your thoughts attempt to simplify situations is through black and white thinking, also known as "all-or-nothing thinking." This can be very limiting and often extreme, especially when there is a whole rainbow of possibilities.

For example: *Sam has a significant amount of social anxiety. Often it is the worst in anticipation of an event. The night before a choir audition, Sam lies awake at night ruminating about the next day. "I'm not going to get the part. I just know the teacher doesn't like me. If I miss a note, everyone will hear it and laugh. I don't know why I'm bothering to audition. I suck. But if I don't try out, my mom will be disappointed and tell me it's too expensive to not even try. I'm never good enough for anything."*

Sam's brain is making a lot of assumptions about what other people think and feel. It makes sense to be nervous before an audition or event. What is important to note is how Sam's brain is creating stories that have not even happened yet, and increasing anxiety for something partially out of their control. Doing so takes away the opportunity of everyone else to show up positively. Sam also demonstrates all-or-nothing thinking when saying NEVER and ALWAYS. This type of thinking eliminates the existence of a neutral or semi-okay experience, only noticing the extremes, either really good or really bad.

The stories you tell yourself on a regular basis become your narrative, the outline for how you interpret the world. In the following exercises you will make note of the common stories you tell yourself, then you will assess the stories for facts. If facts are missing, instead of filling in the blank, you will practice requesting the facts or waiting for them to be revealed. Waiting can be hard when your brain craves instant gratification, but it is necessary to practice patience.

BREAK IT DOWN EXERCISE

BENEFIT: *Breaking down a big task*

TIME: *12 minutes*

Often, life can feel way too big to handle all at once. Decon-
struction is a narrative therapy tool used to narrow down and
simplify the details so you can focus on just a few aspects.
In this exercise you will take an overwhelming situation and
break it down into smaller details to decrease the intensity.

1. Think of a situation coming up that you are feeling overwhelmed about.

   Example: Sam's choir audition.

2. Write down five thoughts that come up that are fueling the anxious feeling.

   "I'm not going to get the part."
   "I just know the teacher doesn't like me."
   "If I miss a note, everyone will hear it and laugh."
   "I don't know why I'm bothering to audition. I suck."
   "If I don't try out, my mom will be disappointed."

3. Choose the three that you have the least control over. Remember, you can't control how other people feel or think.

   "If I miss a note, everyone will hear it and laugh."
   "I just know the teacher doesn't like me."
   "If I don't try out, my mom will be disappointed"

4. Of the three left, choose one that is connected to your own actions.

   "If I miss a note, everyone will hear it and laugh."

5. What step can you take to change this thought or situation?

   Example: Sam can practice more in anticipation of their audition.

6. Continue to break down the steps into even smaller steps.

   Example: Choose specific times, days, and material to practice.

7. When it is something that is out of your control, grant yourself permission to not stress about it until the situation arrives.

QUIZ: ARE YOU AN AVOIDER?

BENEFIT: *Facing the hidden fear*

TIME: *10 minutes*

Avoidance is another common response to overwhelming thoughts. Your brain is trained to identify and avoid the bad. This is a Band-Aid solution that only delays the inevitable. S.T.O.P.-ing to pause and step away (see S.T.O.P. Exercise, page 58) is momentary, whereas avoidance is long-term.

Read through this next quiz of common avoidance statements to explore your coping strategies. If you select "strongly agree," that means your brain shows high levels of avoidance. "Strongly disagree" means your brain doesn't always respond with avoidance. If you use the "sometimes" rating, you're right in the middle. Just be honest, and remember, you're not alone!

(1) STRONGLY DISAGREE (2) SOMETIMES (3) STRONGLY AGREE

1. I won't do something if I think it will make me uncomfortable.

2. When something upsetting comes up, I try very hard to stop thinking about it.

3. I tend to put off unpleasant things that need to get done.

4. Happiness means never feeling any pain or disappointment.

5. I sometimes procrastinate to avoid facing challenges.

6. I work hard to keep out upsetting feelings.

7. I can numb my feelings when they are too intense.

8. I let gloomy thoughts stop me from doing what I want.

9. When a negative thought comes up, I immediately try to think of something else.

10. I try to put off unpleasant tasks for as long as possible.

BALL IN THE POOL EXERCISE

BENEFIT: *Accepting thoughts without criticism*

TIME: *5 minutes*

You've been introduced to intrusive thoughts and avoiding thoughts. Now you will engage in a mindfulness visualization exercise about the impact of forcing and avoiding versus accepting your thoughts. This is an act of acknowledging, accepting, and letting go.

Read through these prompts and notice the difference between avoiding and accepting.

Visualize a beach ball floating in a pool.

The beach ball represents your negative or painful thoughts and emotions you'd rather avoid, and the pool is your mind.

You don't want the beach ball anywhere near you, as it will ruin the day.

You begin pushing the beach ball underwater, away from the surface.

SPLASH! The ball resurfaces. You push it down again, but it floats back to the top again.

It has become a struggle, taking all of your energy. Attempting to avoid the beach ball has become your primary focus.

Try this instead: If you let the beach ball just float around, it may come close or it may move away from you.

Your energy has been redirected away from concealing and trying to control the beach ball and you are focused on the present. You acknowledge the beach ball, accept its presence, and you allow it to move as you enjoy your swim in the pool, unbothered.

Replace the beach ball with a thought and the pool with your mind and see how the story changes!

CHANGING YOUR THOUGHTS

Automatic means you do something without thinking, like fight, flight, or freeze. A learned response is what you are doing right here, right now, learning how to change your thinking about anxiety-producing thoughts. This is who you are choosing to become. Everyone has an internal dialogue, like when you think, "Wait, did I flush the toilet? Oh yeah, I did." The way in which you talk to yourself is very important for your mindfulness practice.

As you explore your internal dialogue and changing your thoughts, there are a few facts to consider:

1. Your mind can control and influence your physical state and brain function.

2. It is easier for your mind to believe negative thoughts over positive ones.

3. Your mind believes the things you tell it.

4. Your mind can't tell the difference between what's real and what's imagined.

5. You are not your thoughts.

Most people have a pretty negative voice, but you are going to change this through what I call "puppy language." If your dog is wandering around off the path you're walking you don't say to them, "Hey, stupid, why can't you stay on the path?" You say, "Hey! Come back this way you little smoosh face." Now translate that to talking to yourself. Instead of, "Why are you so lazy? How could you forget that?" switch it to, "Let's go sleepyhead, time to get started." This change in tone will feel weird at first, but you spend so much time with yourself—why not be the nicest person you interact with?

It is helpful to keep a thought record of both positive and negative experiences. By keeping track of how your mind takes in information, you can start to identify a pattern of how things show up for you, how you respond, what works and doesn't work. The best method is writing it down so you can visually see it. You can do this in a bullet journal, a regular journal, a symptom checklist, or a notes app on your phone. You can also try doing the exercises in this book at different times to see the changes you are making.

The work you are doing here will take time, and the changes will feel tiny at first, but when you are able to look back six months from now, you will see a drastic change in the way you think about your anxiety.

If we can learn to interrupt mindless thinking, we can break out of the shackles of negative loop. The problem is not thinking. It is thinking without knowing that you're thinking.

—JUSTIN SEBASTIAN

 PUPPY MINDFULNESS EXERCISE

BENEFIT: *Reframing negative thoughts*

TIME: *15 minutes*

Using puppy language, explained on page 70, translate these common anxiety thoughts into more positive encouragements. Sometimes going to the other end of an extreme can help you find balance in the middle. Make it silly and extra for added humor. Laughter is the best medicine. Try to translate a few of your own thoughts. The following are common thoughts triggered by anxiety. Read each statement, then rephrase it like how you would say it to a puppy. Practicing this technique will help you use it when you have an automatic negative thought.

EXAMPLE:

"You are too needy, no one wants to be around you."

PUPPY:

"Wow, you know your needs. Let's get them met!"

EXAMPLE:

"I'm so dumb. Why can't I just get this right?"

PUPPY:

"Whoops, haven't gotten it yet. Let's try again!"

1. "Ugh, you are so annoying. No one wants to be around you."

_____

2. "I'm going to sound stupid if I talk in class."

_____

3. "I look awful. I wish I was invisible."

_____

4. "I shouldn't say anything. They'll think I'm a loser."

_____

5. "They'll know I'm faking it."

_____

6. "You're so lazy. Why can't you do anything right?"

_____

7. "Why should I even try? I'll fail anyway."

_____

8. "What's wrong with me?"

_____

9. "I can't go. I'll have a panic attack. No way."

_____

10. "I'm too much. Why bother?"

_____

11. "I'm not capable of doing things alone."

_____

12. "There is nothing I'm good at."

_____

Spend some time hanging out with your pet and notice how you talk to them. Do you talk to them with warmth and compassion? Do you try to laugh and reassure them? Try using that language on yourself, even if it is not a direct translation.

JOURNALING EXERCISE

BENEFIT: *Creating a record of progress*

TIME: *8 minutes*

Taking a moment each day to document your progress is a great way to mindfully reflect on everything you have achieved so far. Use the following prompts and questions to help you track your progress and learn what specifically works for you and what does not. Each day, take a few moments to journal your responses to the prompts and questions. You can use a notebook, a computer, or a notes app on your phone. In six months, you can look back and see how much your thoughts and anxiety have changed.

1. Write the date and time of your entry.

2. One positive moment of the day.

3. One neutral moment of the day.

4. One negative moment of the day.

5. A moment you were able to meet your needs.

6. A struggle you faced by asking for help.

7. What is something you can do today to prepare for a better tomorrow?

8. What is something you can do tomorrow to have a better day?

9. On a scale of 0 to 100, how intense was your anxiety today?

10. Was there someone who was supportive of you today?

Some days will be full of success while other days may be harder. Growth is not a straight line. The hard days will help you recognize where continued support will be of assistance.

CHAPTER 4

Managing Emotions

You are leveling up! In this chapter you'll learn about emotions, the most intense and personal part of the human experience. This topic can get confusing and overwhelming. You are encouraged to move at your own pace. By the time this chapter is over, you will have more insight into the purpose of emotions, how to identify what you are feeling, and ways that you can connect to and shift your emotions. You cannot take away an emotion in its entirety, but you can learn to turn down the volume and decrease the intensity.

EMOTIONAL INTELLIGENCE

There are six universal emotions that can be tracked and identified in every country, culture, and language in the world: anger, sadness, happiness, fear, surprise, and disgust. Each emotion serves an important role in how you connect with the world and people around you. You can also think of each emotion as a different part of yourself that you are getting to know. The more familiar you are with each part, the better you will understand your own triggers. With mindfulness, you will learn to identify which emotion you are feeling, where in your body you are feeling it, what thoughts connect to the emotion, and how to sooth and decrease the intensity.

In her book *Raising Your Emotional Intelligence,* Jeanne Segal defines emotional intelligence as "the ability to understand, use, and manage your own emotions in positive ways to relieve stress, communicate effectively, empathize with others, overcome challenges, and defuse conflict." This also includes emotional vocabulary. The more feeling words you know, the more specifically you can pinpoint and express what is going on inside of you.

The first time you felt anxious, you had no idea what it was. It was scary and overwhelming. Once you knew what to label it as, it made it a bit easier to understand the overflow of emotion. Learning the language and differentiating between emotions will take time and practice.

In most instances, you have a primary emotion that is outwardly expressed and a secondary emotion that is a deeper core feeling. Have you ever snapped at your mom about the chores when really you were hurt that you hadn't heard from a friend? With increased emotional intelligence, your goal is to identify and acknowledge the true feeling under the big emotion. An "umbrella term" is used to refer to a number of subjects that fall into the same category. Picture an open umbrella; the primary feeling is at the top, and the feelings that are contributing to and fueling the primary emotion are under the coverage of the open umbrella. In the example above, anger is primary, although fear, loneliness, sadness, and irritation are also being felt. Once you identify the underlying emotions, you can do more directed work on soothing the secondary emotions.

EMOTIONAL LANGUAGE EXERCISE

BENEFIT: *Expanding emotional vocabulary*

TIME: *20 minutes*

It is time to practice your emotional vocabulary. This activity will test your knowledge of emotional descriptions and categorizations. It's also good to do this with friends or family to introduce them to emotional intelligence. Feeling "fine" will no longer be your only answer.

You will be given an emotional category and a letter. Your job is to write down every word that describes the given category and starts with the given letter.

For example, for emotions that start with M, you would list "mad," "melancholy," and "miserable."

List feelings that begin with S.

_____

What emotions begin with A?

_____

Another word for anger (any letter).

_____

Body sensation beginning with E.

_____

Others words that describe anxiety (any letter).

_____

List sad emotions that begin with D.

_____

Colors you think of that express happiness.

_____

What emotion words would you use to describe school?

_____

List all the positive words you can think of.

_____

Can you think of any emotion words that have not been listed? What category do
they fall into?

_____

EMOTIONAL UMBRELLA EXERCISE

BENEFIT: *Expanding the depth of your own emotional awareness*

TIME: *12 minutes*

What is under your umbrella? Use this exercise to challenge yourself to see beyond the first feeling and identify what the underlying emotions are. This is meant to be difficult. You are getting closer to the core reason behind the intensity of your feelings. Use some of the words from the Emotional Language exercise on page 82 to be more specific.

1. Get out a pen and paper.

2. Draw an umbrella. Seeing it on paper gives a new perspective.

3. Think of a recent situation when an emotion was overwhelming. Write this emotion at the top of the umbrella. This is the primary emotion.

4. Think about why this situation made you feel this way.

5. Start with a sentence, then shorten it to one summarizing word.

6. Then, identify at least three other words connected to the primary emotion. Write these under the umbrella. These are the secondary emotions.

7. Pick one of the secondary emotion words. Can you think of an emotion that fuels this feeling?

8. With your pen, connect the primary emotion, secondary emotions, and secondary emotion word that you singled out. This is a pattern you experience in your life. The situation triggered a series of emotions.

9. The last emotion word is the core emotion to focus your healing on. Typically, this emotion word has to do with worth, value, or being enough.

WHO DOES THIS EMOTION BELONG TO?

Now that you know how to name emotions, you can start identifying what they may be connected to. There are times you will intensely feel an emotion but have no idea where it is coming from or what triggered it. Hypervigilance is an intensified need to seek and scan for safety. This can look like hypersensitivity, or becoming overly aware of others' feelings and emotions because you are scanning the situation to proactively guard your own emotions. When you have a close relationship and are connected to someone (family, friend, partner), typically you can pick up on how they are feeling. Example: *Dad walks in after work, and instantly, without a word spoken, you just know he is in a bad mood.* Having this awareness is essentially good, as you can use the skill to gauge situations and know who are safe people for you. It can also be called a gut reaction or intuition.

When you experience trauma or have anxiety, your gauge of safety can be skewed, meaning you over- or underreact to your emotions. People are most aware of their negative emotions: sadness, depression, disappointment, loneliness, anger, frustration, and irritability. It is absolutely okay to feel and express being sad or mad. They are natural emotions. They are also the emotions you may have the hardest time sitting with if someone else is expressing anger or sadness.

Consider this example: *Jess walks to the park to meet a couple of friends. As soon as they join the group, a weird vibe can be felt; it's quiet and awkward. Jess's first thought is, "They don't want me here," and they start to feel anxious and insecure. A few minutes later, Quin shares with Jess that he was just broken up with and had just finished telling the story. Now it makes sense to Jess why it felt so odd joining the group at that moment. Jess picked up on the mix of sadness and frustration the group was experiencing, and this triggered their own fears of feeling unwanted.*

In this example, you can see how individual and group emotions can become mixed and influence your own feelings. The better you know your own emotions, the easier it is to sort out what are theirs and what are yours. Then you can remind yourself, "This emotion isn't mine!" If it is not yours, you do not need to hold on to it or solve it. You are only responsible for your emotions.

 NAME IT, TAME IT EXERCISE

BENEFIT: *Learning to name an emotion to have more control*

TIME: *5 minutes*

Do you remember a time you were anxious, and people kept asking what was wrong, but you didn't know, so you couldn't tell them? And as they kept asking you, you kept getting more anxious? Being able to identify your emotions will help tease out whether your feelings belong to you or someone else. The first time you do this activity, use a past event to practice. Reflect on a journal entry from the Journaling Exercise in chapter 3 (page 76).

1. Get out your journal and a pen and choose an entry.

2. Think back to the specific experience. What were you feeling? Write it down on a new page in your journal.

3. Then, using a different-color pen, identify and label the emotions connected to your memory of the situation.

4. Do this for each question you answered in the entry. It is okay to list multiple feelings for each answer.

5. Notice how naming the emotion adds more depth and clarity to the situation.

6. Repeat the exercise, except this time write down descriptive emotion words for your present feeling.

The more frequently you practice naming your emotions, the easier it will become in the moment to self-identify your feelings and what you need to take care of yourself.

BLENDING EMOTIONS QUIZ

BENEFIT: *Identifying mixed emotions*

TIME: *10 minutes*

Yes, you can feel more than one emotion at once! Sometimes they are separate and sometimes they create a whole new emotion. Often, the reason emotions feel incredibly overwhelming is because you are feeling multiple emotions at once. You've already worked on naming your emotions; now you will identify how some emotions go hand in hand. Two emotions will be listed, and your task is to identify the new emotion that the two create. Reference the list of emotions you created with the Emotional Language Exercise on page 82.

Mad + Sad = *Hurt*

Happy + Sad + Mad + Afraid + Disgusted + Surprised = *Overwhelmed*

Sad + Surprised = _____

Happy + Sad = _____

Afraid + Mad = _____

Surprised + Happy = _____

Happy + Afraid = _____

Nervous + Sad = _____

Afraid + Sad = _____

Disgusted + Mad = _____

Mad + Surprised = _____

Feel free to add a few of your own!

_____

_____

_____

Remix! For each emotion listed, identify what two emotions create it.

Irritable = _____ + _____

Jealous = _____ + _____

Lonely = _____ + _____

Bitter = _____ + _____

Nervous = _____ + _____

Doubtful = _____ + _____

Excited = _____ + _____

Anxious = _____ + _____

Disappointed = _____ + _____

*Assign an emotion to each color of a color wheel, then
see what color the two blended emotions would make!*

☀ "I FEEL . . ." EXERCISE

BENEFIT: *Clear communication about feelings*

TIME: *5 minutes*

When you start a statement with "*You* make me . . ." the other person automatically goes on defense, which makes the whole conversation unproductive. The goal with mindfulness is to take ownership of your own emotions. You are going to practice creating "I feel" statements to acknowledge your feelings and address how another person contributed. You are not putting responsibility on them; rather, you are connecting how their actions triggered your emotions. The following is a script that you can practice using to express your emotions.

"I feel (emotion) when you (action), because it makes me feel (emotion).

I would prefer if (your request)."

EXAMPLE:

"I feel irritated when you speak over me, because it makes me feel unimportant.

I would prefer if you'd let me finish my thought and then share yours."

1. Write out this script and think of a situation in which it was difficult for you to verbally express how you were feeling to someone. You won't be sharing this with them, it is just practice.

2. A script can feel awkward and unnatural the first time it is spoken. Just as actors must practice their lines, the more you incorporate "I feel" statements into your language, the easier it will flow.

3. Use this script while journaling to help sort out where your emotions come from. If you feel overwhelmed and don't know what to say, step away and write it out so your thoughts are clear before expressing them.

MAKING FRIENDS WITH YOUR EMOTIONS

You are aware of how emotions can be intense, overwhelming, and negative. Because of this, there is a natural tendency to avoid them, put on a mask, hide, and say, "I'm fine." Alternatively, you can become friends with your emotions. Sit down with your anxiety and ask where it came from, what brings it to you today, and how you can help. Acknowledge your emotions as a part of you that is actively changing, and not the definition of who you are. It makes anxiety feel less daunting when you can engage with your emotions rather than being taken over by them.

anxiety holds me hostage inside of my house, inside of my head.

Mom says where did anxiety come from?

anxiety is the cousin visiting from out of town

depression felt obligated to bring to the party.

Mom, i am the party.

—SABRINA BENAIM, "EXPLAINING
MY DEPRESSION TO MY MOTHER: A CONVERSATION"

Emotions are not easy to verbally express and articulate. There are ways to express and share your feelings through nonverbal communication. When you are feeling stuck and struggling to name it, feel free to connect with yourself and others in alternative ways. Music is an incredible tool for feeling and expressing emotion. When you listen to a song, the instruments can be felt in your body. There is validation in an artist speaking your thoughts out loud. The realization that hundreds or millions of other people have connected with the same song can suddenly make you feel less alone. Art is a powerful tool of expression, and many artists rely on the intensity of their emotions to create deeply felt work: from poetry to painting, from memes to comedy, from sketches to novels. The way you express yourself can be uniquely yours, and/or a way to connect with others. Maybe you can give a voice to your own and others' emotions through your own creativity.

Think about the activities you enjoy the most when you feel yourself, neutral, and happy. When do you feel confident, excited, and capable? Whatever this activity is, this is your strength. Don't worry if you aren't any good at it. What matters is that you feel connected to yourself while doing it. For many people, just seeing someone they love happy and excited about a preferred topic is exciting for that very reason. These are the tools you can expand upon and utilize to self soothe and ground yourself.

PLAYLIST EXERCISE

BENEFIT: *Having a playlist ready for any feeling*

TIME: *30 minutes*

Music is a powerful way to connect to your emotions. The music can join you in whatever state you are in. It can even change your mood. Have you ever been down, but then your favorite song plays, and suddenly your body is moving to the beat? Music has the power to put emotions into words that speak from the soul. It is proof that you are not alone in the feelings you are having; someone else felt the same way and wrote a song about it! The goal of this exercise is to create separate playlists for different emotional needs. By making the lists now, they will be ready for you whenever you need them.

1. Make a playlist for when you are feeling (insert emotion) and want to remain in that mood.

2. As you are listening to the songs, notice what body sensations arise.

3. Notice any thoughts or memories that pop into your head.

4. Do you connect to the sound, beat, or instruments? Is it different depending on the genre?

5. Pay attention to the lyrics. How do the words highlight the emotion you are feeling?

6. As you listen to additional songs, does your mood change?

Challenge yourself to make a playlist to change your emotion. If you are sad, are there specific songs that bring a smile to your face?

PERSONAL TOOLBOX EXERCISE

BENEFIT: *Centralizing your preferred tools*

TIME: *10 minutes*

A toolbox is where you keep the skills you have learned and thoughts that you've gathered regarding your mindfulness practice. Your toolbox can be literal or figurative—either way, it is a centralized place to keep an inventory of what works for you in moments of anxiety. It is your go-to place for self-soothing and healing. Each of these options is helpful when you become overwhelmed by an emotion, because when you are in fight, flight, or freeze mode, it can be difficult to think of what helped you last time.

On a piece of paper, make a list of the mindfulness strategies that you personally feel connected to.

Be specific with your list. Instead of writing "breathe," write "take five breaths."

Hang the list in a place that you see daily (for example, on a mirror, door, or nightstand). The purpose of making the list visible is so you don't have to think of or remember what to do.

Now when you are triggered, you have a "to-do list" of actions that help you feel better.

OPTION 2:

Use a pencil bag as your toolbox.

Put items in the bag that help support you in self-soothing (for example, a fidget toy, essential oil, or a picture of your dog).

Keep the bag within easy reach in your backpack, purse, or nightstand.

When you become triggered, you won't have to think about what makes you feel better. You'll just reach for your bag of items to help ground yourself.

CHAPTER 5

Challenging Your Behaviors

As you've learned, emotions lead to thoughts, and thoughts lead to behaviors. Now let's explore how your anxiety is manifesting as behaviors in your current life. Once you can identify them, then you can add in mindfulness and adjust for your comfort. Many behaviors are comforting and self-soothing at first but can often lead to avoidance and may become limiting.

This chapter will identify why anxiety appears in behaviors, how to incorporate your mindfulness skills, and new actions to help you stay emotionally regulated.

YOU CAN'T HIDE FROM YOUR ANXIETY

People naturally find ways to cope with their anxiety. Anxious behaviors can look like physical soothing, such as pacing, leg shaking, and skin picking, or can be an action, like leaving, avoiding, and withdrawing. As these behaviors are addressed, keep in mind that all of them are acceptable occasionally, but not all the time. Thoughts and emotions can be automatic. Behaviors typically have a thought and choice behind them, although you can engage in a behavior so frequently that it feels like you do it without thinking, such as scratching an itch.

Anxious behaviors are typically rooted in self-soothing, which we discussed in chapter 2 as ways to use your body to help regulate your anxiety. It can feel like energy or emotion needs to be released from your body, so you may find yourself pacing a room, constantly shaking your leg, or fidgeting with your hands, hair, or clothing. You do not have to force yourself to stop; you just need to shift the connection between thought and action. If you unconsciously pick at your nails or cuticles, try a fidget ring or beaded bracelet instead. Anxious behaviors are not bad—they just need a little adjustment to increase how helpful they are.

Some actions start out as helpful but can turn into negative behaviors if continued. For example, it's okay to leave an overwhelming environment, but if you do it every time, it can shift and morph into avoidance, becoming harder to address in time. Due to fear, your comfort zone will become smaller and smaller, trapping you in your head. If you can navigate through the fear zone, you'll find the learning zone, followed by growth, and then just like that, your comfort zone expands. Exposure therapy is one way to challenge avoidance behaviors. You slowly and incrementally increase interaction with the feared situation or thing as you aim to build familiarity and comfort. However, you DO NOT have to become comfortable with dangerous, threatening, or toxic situations. Not everything should be tolerated.

The following exercises will support you in challenging your comfort zone and help you shift anxious behaviors toward a more mindful approach. As you reflect on your habits, ask yourself if they are impacting your ability to connect or experience things in your life. If your answer is "yes," then these exercises are for you.

We change our behavior when the pain of staying the same becomes greater than the pain of changing.

—DR. HENRY CLOUD

SLOW IT DOWN EXERCISE

BENEFIT: *Intentional release of energy*

TIME: *3 minutes*

Have you ever had someone ask you to stop shaking your leg, and you didn't even know you were doing it? This is a mindLESS action. When you do notice, you can switch to mindFULness by slowing down the motion and checking in with your body's needs in that moment. For this exercise, you will perform a repetitive action and be guided to mindfully engage with the same action.

1. Begin with a brief scan of your body. Are you fidgeting? Fidgeting looks like:

   Leg tapping

   Playing with a pen

   Picking at your fingers

2. Bring attention to your (insert your most common fidget).

3. Decrease the speed of the motion. Notice the flex of your muscle. Notice the impact of the ground. Notice new sensations that appear. Sensations feel like:

   An urge or need to go faster

   A release

   Shame, embarrassment, humor

4. Slow it down a bit more. Notice any sensations, thoughts, and emotions again.

5. Return to the original movement. Check in with your sensations, thoughts, and emotions.

6. What did you like or dislike about this exercise? Any answer will give you more insight into what is or is not helpful for you.

7. Repeat the exercise throughout the day and see if your experience shifts.

8. When you do something mindlessly, it typically does not meet the desired need. By incorporating mindful awareness, you can receive the sensory input or release of energy that is needed to decrease your anxiety.

FIND YOUR COMFORT ZONE EXERCISE

BENEFIT: *Identifying areas where you can safely challenge your fears*

TIME: *10 minutes*

You already know what you are comfortable doing, and you've identified triggers in previous exercises. Now you are going to stretch your comfort zone by zooming in on the fine line between comfort and fear, the space in which things become challenging. In this exercise, you will create a visual representation of your comfort zone.

1. Draw four columns on a blank piece of paper. At the top, label them: "Situation," "Comfort," "Challenge," and "Fear."

2. In the *Situation* column, list an event that is difficult for you to engage in. (Example: public speaking.)

3. Under *Comfort*, identify the level to which you are comfortable approaching the situation. (Example: in situations with less than 10 people, with people who you are familiar with, or with a familiar topic.)

4. For *Challenge*, brainstorm and identify something that could be just beyond comfortable but not enough to make you start to panic. (Example: 12 people, mixed group of familiar people, an easy but new topic.)

5. In the *Fear* column, identify the absolute limit of what you would be capable of doing. (Example: 50 people, a classroom full of high school seniors, a completely unknown topic.)

Review the Challenge column. If you believe that it is realistic, push yourself a bit more. It's okay if it feels like too much to take on all at once. Try to break it down into smaller increments that are easier to accomplish. Do this with each anxiety-producing situation, and again every time you conquer a previous fear. If you do, your comfort zone will continue to expand!

STAYING CONNECTED

Anxiety can also lead to disengaging from the world by withdrawing or pulling back from friends and family when your mental health declines. People often do this to hide their own pain, out of fear of feeling like a burden, or from embarrassment. Disconnecting may seem necessary when the brain feels overwhelmed with emotion and wants to protect itself.

Unfortunately, too much alone time and isolation can make the pain worse and trigger heavier, sadder feelings. This can look like wearing an emotional mask—being someone else on the outside while hiding your true emotions to portray another feeling instead. People are more likely to pretend to be okay than to fake mental health struggles.

So, how do you take off the mask and feel capable of sharing your true experience? Becoming more aware of how your anxiety affects you mentally and physically will help. Learning more about the ways to talk about anxiety and how you're feeling—or improving your emotional vocabulary—will help, too. Lastly, learning what your anxiety triggers are will help you increase your confidence day by day. By working through this book you'll improve your ability to clearly articulate and share your experiences.

Let's look at an example of mask on versus mask off:

Friend: Hey! How are you? Where have you been?

Mask On: *Hey! I'm fine, just been busy.*

Friend: Do you want to hang out this weekend?

Mask On.*: I wish I could! I already have plans, though.*

Friend: Darn, I miss hanging out with you.

Mask On.*: I miss hanging out with you, too! We'll have to plan something soon.*

This next example is a little different as it touches on being upfront and honest, but focusing on painful times.

Friend: Hey! How are you? Where've you been?

Mask Off: *Hey, not great. It's been hard lately.*

Friend: Oh wow, I thought something was off. Do you want to hang out this weekend?

Mask Off: *Hmm, no thanks. Too many people overwhelm me.*

Friend: What if it was just me and you?

Mask Off.*: Actually, that might be nice.*

Do you notice the difference between the two conversations? In one, the person kept their mask on and kept their friend at a distance. Compare that to the second conversation, where being honest and clear about their reality opened space for the friend to offer support in a way that was helpful. What would it be like to be upfront about what you are experiencing? It would be very vulnerable and revealing! The instinct is to keep everything to yourself and figure out a way to deal with your emotions on your own. We've learned that isn't the best path to take! You'd be surprised at the number of people that are feeling exactly what you are feeling. There is real community in connecting with others, even if it is regarding shared struggle. Remember the phrase "name it to tame it" from chapter 1 (page 2)? Your friends and family may not know how to show up for you if they don't know what is going on inside of you. Try taking off the mask and allowing others to see your true self.

 VULNERABILITY IS . . . QUIZ

BENEFIT: *Identifying how okay you are with being vulnerable*

TIME: *5 minutes*

Are there areas of life you are more comfortable sharing with people? You might find it easier to share facts rather than emotions. Take this quiz to identify areas that are easy or hard for you to share with others. Identify the feelings and emotions that come up as you respond to each question. What are you feeling and where are you feeling it? Were these habits directly taught to you, or did you pick them up subtly from others? Knowing where your hesitancy comes from allows you to more clearly understand how to take it apart.

Respond to each of the following with either "Yes," "No," or "Sometimes."

Are you emotionally vulnerable? _____

Do you cry in front of others? _____

Do you struggle expressing your emotions? _____

Have you been heartbroken? _____

Were you taught that showing emotions or vulnerability makes you weak?

_____

Are you afraid of others' reactions to your vulnerability?

_____

Do you feel like others won't be supportive of you?

_____

Do you keep people at arm's length for your protection?

_____

How does that play a role in allowing yourself to be vulnerable with others?

_____

Do you know how and when to trust others? _____

Do you hide your true feelings, positive or negative?

_____

What have you learned about your own vulnerability? Write that down here.

_____

_____

_____

# CREATE A MASK EXERCISE

BENEFIT: *Learning to match your internal feelings to your external emotions*
TIME: *20 minutes*

Creating a visual representation of your emotions, thoughts, and feelings is a great way to get out of your head and see what is going on. This is a practice of externalizing—taking something you experience inside and bringing it outside of yourself.

1. Assemble a few supplies: blank paper and writing utensils, like markers or colored pens.

2. Choose one side of the paper to represent the face that you show the world. It is the "I'm okay" face that you put on to get through the day.

   Write words, adjectives, and descriptions:
   How would you describe this side?
   How would others describe you?
   Use different colors:
   Bright colors: You pretend to be happy and bright
   Muted colors: Hiding in plain sight
   Dark colors: You show sadness/pain
   Add shapes, images, and stickers.

3. Side two will represent the parts of you that only you know. It will consist of the parts of you that you hide from others and that are harder to share.

   Write words, adjectives, and descriptions:
   How would you describe this side?
   How would others describe you?
   Use different colors:
   Bright colors: You feel happy and energetic
   Muted colors: Blah, neutral
   Dark colors: Sadness, pain
   Add shapes, images, and stickers.

4. Now look at both sides. Is there a difference? If so, try the Find Your Comfort Zone Exercise (page 108) to see if you can share more.

PUTTING ALL THE PIECES TOGETHER EXERCISE

BENEFIT: *Combining your skills and self-regulating*

TIME: *5 minutes*

The earlier you can start noticing a change in your mood, the sooner you can implement a coping skill and decrease the anxious experience before it even gets started. This exercise is a mix of physical soothing, guided imagery, and deep breathing. Read through the instructions and then find a comfortable seat, close your eyes, and follow each step.

1. Cross your arms on your chest, placing each hand on the opposite shoulder.

2. Alternate rhythmically tapping your hands on your shoulders: left, right, left, right.

3. Think of a place where you feel calm; it can be a place you have visited, somewhere you dream of going, or a fictional location.

4. Continue tapping and breathe deeply, in through your nose and out your mouth.

5. Continue tapping and close your eyes. Visualize the calm place.

6. Continue tapping and breathe deeply, in through your nose and out your mouth.

7. Notice every detail: each sound, smell, and texture in the room.

8. Continue tapping and breathe deeply, in through your nose and out your mouth.

9. Once you take in every detail and feel relaxed, you may bring yourself back into the room you are currently sitting in.

10. Open your eyes and take a deep breath.

11. Take an inventory of how you are now feeling.

The more frequently you do this exercise, the more quickly you can achieve the relaxing results.

CYCLE BREAKER

Many of the ways you manage your emotions are learned from those around you. It is a combination of societal expectations, social pressures, and family structure. Maybe you are the first in your family or group to talk about mental health and are paving the way for others to speak out about their experiences. You are a Cycle Breaker shining light on the importance of mental health. You may have family members who are stuck in anxiety, and you've picked up their habits. You are a Cycle Breaker creating new habits, behaviors, and cycles for yourself as well as for your family. When one person makes a major change, there is a ripple effect that causes others to notice the positive impact and then choose to make major life changes as well. By doing the mindfulness work in this book, you are a Cycle Breaker. This means you are breaking out of the continuous cycle of things remaining the same. This is an awesome role to take on; it is hard, but it is so healing.

There will be times when others are not supportive of the new actions and habits you are practicing. Not everyone is comfortable with change, and the changes you are making are big. The goal is to disrupt the system that created and perpetuated your anxiety. If you stay true to yourself and your values, and do no harm to yourself or others, then you are on the right path whether people agree with you or not.

Maintaining motivation is often difficult when faced with an uphill challenge. Remember why you are putting all this effort into managing your anxiety: to feel better, to be able to do things, to connect with other people. Take a moment to think about a quote or a phrase that connects to your experience and where you want to be. The quote can be from a movie, song, or book. Use the quote as a mantra to anchor yourself and help you keep striving forward. Think of all the information you have learned so far and the exercises you have practiced. Building the skills into your everyday actions creates a new pattern of behaviors that will lead to a mindful approach to your life. The changes you are making are not a one-time cure-all; they are best practiced regularly. This is an active process of unlearning and relearning how to approach and manage everyday obstacles.

SELF-CARE EXERCISE

BENEFIT: *Surrounding yourself with positive supports*

TIME: *10 minutes*

Self-care happens throughout the day, every day. There are little moments that you can incorporate into each day to help you cope, de-stress, and regulate your emotions. It is helpful to identify what they are so you can mindfully practice, even if just for a moment. Everyone has a few routines or specific ways they like to go about a task. Create a list of small actions or moments already present in your day that support your feeling good; if good is too hard, then create a list for "okay" or "neutral." Next are a few prompts to explore some self-care routines people commonly do without realizing it.

How do you start your morning routine?

Shower (fresh/clean)

Outfit (comfort/self-expression)

Breakfast (wake up/energy)

What do you take to school with you to feel prepared?

Water bottle (hydration)

Charged phone (connection/distraction)

Sweatshirt (warmth/comfort)

Do you have a lunch routine?

Where do you meet your friends?

Do you bring food or get it at school?

What do you do after school?

Do you take a break? (Alone or with others?)

Is there something you specifically do to relax?

What is your evening routine?

Hanging out with a pet/sibling/friend

Spending time listening to music

How do you prepare for bedtime?

Choosing comfy pajamas

Saying good night

How do you relax to fall asleep?

As you go about your daily routine, pay extra attention to how each thing makes you feel. Staying mindful will help decrease the stress buildup of the day.

DAILY MANTRA EXERCISE

BENEFIT: *Active reminder of how capable you are*

TIME: *8 minutes*

A mantra is a simple phrase to remind yourself what you are capable of. Having one to repeat to yourself will support you when you take on hard or challenging situations. Your mantra can change based on the situation or how you are feeling.

Read the following suggestions aloud. As you do, listen to what your gut tells you is right for you. Pick a few that feel like a good fit and incorporate saying them into your daily routine.

I choose to trust myself and others.

I can adapt and thrive on my own.

I choose to survive and thrive.

I choose to be in charge of my life.

I choose to be myself.

I deserve love.

I accept that I am a good person.

I choose to be okay as I am.

I am doing my best.

I am worthy.

I am proud of myself.

I will not worry about things I cannot control.

I am on my side.

I define my worth and I am worthy.

I like who I am becoming.

I deserve time to recharge.

My past has shaped me into something wonderful.

You may have heard a mantra you like that is not listed. Take a moment to think of your own that specifically fits you. You can start by stating a fact about yourself and work up to the positive.

I am a student.

I am _____

I choose to start my day.

I choose _____

I accept I am here today.

I accept _____

I will have a _____ day.

Now think of a few that are unique to you. Write them down here.

_____

_____

_____

_____

_____

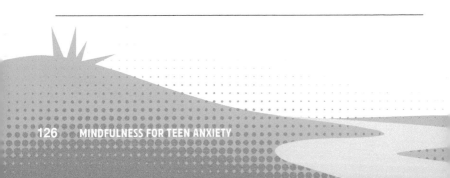

CONCLUSION

Congratulations! You've made it through so much information, completed numerous challenging exercises, and discovered new ways of thinking. As you put your knowledge into action, remember "progress over perfection." The goal is not to be anxiety free; it is to become in tune with what anxiety is trying to tell you and how to regulate your experience. As your life evolves and changes, so will your emotions and needs. You may experience another period of intense anxiety, but you are never starting over with your practice, just starting again in a new place. Being more mindful comes with more mindfulness practice. Everyone is unique, so take what works for you and leave what does not. You are a capable, worthy, and valuable person. Now go out there and take on the world.

Books

Brown, Brené. *Daring Greatly: How the Courage to Be Vulnerable Transforms the Way We Live, Love, Parent, and Lead.* New York: Penguin, 2012.
A book to increase comfort about taking risks, accessing shame, and vulnerability.

Coelho, Paulo. *The Alchemist.* New York: HarperOne, 1993.
A story of a young boy seeking his life's purpose, and the colorful characters he meets along the way.

Siegel, Dr. Daniel J. *The Mindful Brain: Reflection and Attunement in the Cultivation of Well-Being.* New York: W. W. Norton & Company, 2007.
Written by a phenomenal neuroscientist that focuses on brain development and mindfulness.

Tawwab, Nedra Glover. *Set Boundaries, Find Peace: A Guide to Reclaiming Yourself.* New York: TarcherPerigee, 2021.
Learn how to set clear and firm boundaries with people you care about to have healthy relationships.

van der Kolk, Bessel. *The Body Keeps the Score: Brain, Mind, and Body in the Healing of Trauma.* New York: Penguin, *2014.*
A look at how the body holds and processes trauma.

Websites

MindfulnessForTeens.com – Resource center for teens looking for additional information on mindfulness.

TED.com – Brief videos by experts in psychology, mindfulness, and the brain (as well as every other topic imaginable) that are intended to spark new ideas.

KatiMorton.com – A YouTuber and LMFT who shares insightful information about coping with mental health struggles.

Apps

Headspace – A mindfulness meditation app with hundreds of guided meditations, daily affirmations, and self-soothing tools.

Calm – A guided meditation app with an emphasis on improving quality of sleep.

REFERENCES

Anxiety & Depression Association of America. "Teens /College Students." Accessed September 2021. ADAA.org /find-help/by-demographics/teens-college-students?g-clid=Cj0KCQjw1dGJBhD4ARIsANb6OdlVPvKqOiM txijeZPneCpTsoigmW-dyfXf4MOwCysSU4GxXiA21 mFkaAp4rEALw_wcB.

Association Zen Internationale. "History of Zen Buddhism." Accessed September 2021. Zen-Azi.org /en/history-zen-buddhism.

Benaim, Sabrina. "explaining my depression to my mother: a conversation." *Depression & Other Magic Tricks*. Minneapolis, MN: Button Poetry. 2017.

Brown, Brene. *The Gift of Imperfection*. Center City, MN: Hazelden Publishing, 2010.

Cloud, Henry, and John Townsend. *Boundaries Leader's Guide*. Grand Rapids, MI: Zondervan, 1999.

Doyle, Glennon. *Untamed*. New York: The Dial Press, 2020.

Ecuza, Nikola. "I'm a bad person." Tumblr. Posted November 5, 2015.

Frankl, Viktor E. *Man's Search for Meaning*. Boston, MA: Beacon Press, 2006.

Gámez, Wakiza, Michael Chmielewski, Roman Kotov, and Camilo Ruggero. "The Brief Experiential Avoidance Questionnaire: Development and Initial Validation." Psychological Assessment 26, no. 1 (March 2014): 35–45. doi: 10.1037/a0034473.

Gawdat, Mo. "Solve for Happy: Engineer Your Path to Joy." March 21, 2017. Gallery Books.

Harris, Sara. "Reframing Our Thoughts to Have Positive Feelings." All Health Network. February 10, 2021. Accessed January 2022. Allhealthnetwork.org/colorado-spirit /reframing-our-thoughts-to-have-positive-feelings.

Hazel. "10 Science-Based Facts That Will Change the Way You Think." Mind Cafe. June 15, 2020. Accessed January 2022. Medium.com/mind-cafe/10-science-based-facts-that -will-change-the-way-you-think-c207a4e8b22.

Kabat-Zinn, Jon. "About the Author." Guided Mindfulness Meditation Practices with Jon Kabat-Zinn. Accessed September 2021. MindfulnessCDs.com/pages/about -the-author.

Muskin, Philip R. "What Are Anxiety Disorders?" American Psychiatric Association. June 2021. Psychiatry.org /patients-families/anxiety-disorders/what-are -anxiety-disorders.

Nicolls, Maryanne. "7 Pillars of Mindfulness." The Joy of Living. Accessed September 2021. TheJoyOfLiving.co /tag/7-pillars-of-mindfulness.

Rane, Zulie. "Confessions of a Bad Feminist." *Zulie Rane* (blog). January 5, 2019. Zulie.Medium.com/confessions -of-a-bad-feminist-96849ec7724b.

Saddiqi, Ayesha. Twitter post. May 15, 2013, 3:11 p.m. Twitter .com/ayeshaasiddiqi/status/334747947222855680?lang=en.

Segel, Jeanne, Melinda Smith, Lawrence Robinson, and Jennifer Shubin. "Improving Emotional Intelligence (EQ)." Help Guide. July 2021. Accessed October 2021. HelpGuide .org/articles/mental-health/emotional-intelligence-eq.htm.

Verma, Prakhar. "300+ Emotions and Feelings." Design Epic Life. Accessed October 2021. DesignEpicLife.com /list-of-emotions.

INDEX

R

*Raising Your Emotional
    Intelligence* (Segal), 80
Reframing, 57
Relaxation exercises
  body scan, 52–53
  tense and release, 40–41

S

Segal, Jeanne, 80
Self-awareness, 4, 19
Self-care, 122–123
Self-regulation exercise,
    118–119
Separation anxiety, 8
Siegal, Daniel, 2, 42
Social anxiety/phobia, 7
Soothing behaviors, 104–105
S.T.O.P. exercise, 58–59
Strength-based therapy, 12
Support systems, 11–13

T

Tapping exercise, 119
Therapy modalities, 12–13
Thoughts
  avoidance quiz, 66–67
  ball in the pool
      exercise, 68–69
  brain development
      and, 56–57

break it down exercise, 64–65
dysfunctional thought
    record exercise, 60–61
mental anxiety
    symptoms, 9–10
mind-body connection,
    26–27, 36–37, 48–49
reframing, 57, 70–74
S.T.O.P. exercise, 58–59
types of, 62–63
Trauma, 86
Triggers
  identifying, 8–9
  flight, flight, or freeze, 42–43
  quiz, 14–16
Trust, 24

U

Umbrella terms, 81, 84–85

V

Visualization, 49–51
Vulnerability, 114–115

W

"Window of tolerance"
    state, 42–43

Z

Zen Buddhism, 22

ACKNOWLEDGMENTS

I would like to acknowledge and thank the people who encouraged, supported, and rallied me through the long nights of writing. To the fearsome foursome—the ones who remind me to be mindful, to my UCLA family, to the women who became sisters, and to my actual family. All of you have kept me afloat in the darkness and celebrated with me in the light. I am forever grateful for your love.

ABOUT THE AUTHOR

 **Jamie D. Roberts** (she/her) is a Licensed Marriage and Family Therapist and founder of Equilibrium Counseling Services, a teen mental health center. Her counseling center is a welcoming and validating atmosphere for every race, spiritual affiliation, sexual orientation, and gender seeking to become a Cycle Breaker by prioritizing their own mental health. As a queer neurodivergent therapist, she understands and celebrates the intersection of identities and the impact this has on one's own mental health. Jamie describes her work as strength based with the goal of building upon innate qualities to navigate through life's obstacles. Outside of work Jamie spends her free time hosting mindfulness paint nights, traveling, and playing with her two kitties, Zeus and Athena.